Beautiful America's

Washington

Happy Birthday,
my dearest David!
May my Washington become
as beautiful to you as your England
is to me!
I love you!
Your own,
Sharon

Front Cover/Craig Tuttle

Published by
Beautiful America Publishing Co.
9725 S.W. Commerce Circle
Wilsonville, Oregon 97070
Revised Second Edition 1990

Library of Congress Cataloging-in-Publication Data
Beautiful America's Washington

1. Washington (State) — Description and travel — 1981 —
Views.
2. Natural history — Washington (State) — Pictorial
works.
[1. Washington (State) — Description and travel.
2. Natural history — Washington (State)]
F892.S84   1987   917.97   87-11490
ISBN 0-89802-491-9
ISBN 0-89802-490-0 (paperback)

Craig Tuttle

Beautiful America's
Washington

Text by Linda Sterling-Wanner

Contents

Introduction

As they entered the strange new land, hope mingled with apprehension. Could it be as they had been led to believe? They saw that the waters were pure and its forests seemed protective.

They passed their first day on the beach gathering geoduck clams for supper. In front of the large driftwood fire they built that evening, they pried the large white shells open and hungrily pulled out the succulent meat. She spoke quietly then of the beauty of the place, but his attention wandered, for he was considering what the canoe trip inland would be like. Tomorrow their travels would begin once more.

The scene I speak of could have occurred 100 years ago—or yesterday. Such are the delights of Washington, unchanging in the ways that make it an appealing vacationland for tourists and cause it to be a continued blessing for those who call it home. While it is a progressive state, it has somehow managed to remain almost timeless in its natural beauty.

Washington is a state of geographic diversity. During the Cenozoic Era the earth twisted and folded and erupted into the formation of today's Coastal Range. Over time, sediments and lava flowed to form an arc-shaped basin known today as the Willamette Valley-Puget Sound basin. Ice-age glaciers appeared and soon left their offspring clinging among the mountains and valleys of the Cascades. Over sixty of these ice-age children still nestle there to create the largest settlement of active glaciers in the U.S. outside of Alaska.

This same great Cascade Range divides the state into a western one-third which has some of the highest rainfalls in the United States and an eastern two-thirds that contains large desert areas, protected by the great shadow of the Cascades. Thus emerge the diversities of production. Western Washington works at forest and sea-related industries coupled with substantial manufacturing. Eastern Washington is largely agricultural. Wheat, fruits, vegetables, and

Mt. Rainier Wilderness/Craig Tuttle

Mt. Shuksan/Craig Tuttle

7

livestock are brought moisture by vast irrigation projects. These projects are a result of taming the once wild Columbia River. The tamers of the river left in their path a stairway of placid lakes that support growth on the otherwise arid plateaus of Eastern Washington. Washington, in fact, leads all the states in hydroelectric generation.

With more than 200 species of edible fish and shellfish off her coasts, Washington leads the West Coast in the processing and distribution of seafoods. Agriculture is also imporant to Washington's economy, as is livestock. Dairy cattle are raised predominantly in the west and northeast, and beef cattle graze the ranges of Central Washington. The state ranks first in the United States for aluminum production.

Though rainfall is high in some areas and almost nonexistent in others, Washington's climate is known as "humid mesothermal." Translated, that means delightfully cool summers and mild winters for the Washington populace. Indeed, its climate is milder than that of any other state at the same latitude because of protection from cold Canadian arctic air by the Rockies.

This temperate climate contributes to making Washington a mecca for sports enthusiasts. Boats of every size and shape are available including catamarans, canoes, kayaks, and ferries. White water rafting, windsurfing, swimming, and beachcombing are popular, too. And as the terrain provides the mountains, forests, and fields for it, camping, backpacking, and hiking are popular pastimes. Over a thousand lakes and rivers exist and 2,500 miles of shoreline can be measured. With five national parks, six national forests, and 101 state parks, Washington has a plethora of natural wonders available.

Among the top attractions are fishing for salmon, tuna, and bottom fish on the coast, and fresh water fishing for trout, bass, and steelhead. A dozen major ski resorts offer skiing and related wintertime activities. Sight-seeing alone is a popular draw. Professional baseball, basketball, football, hockey, rodeo, and volleyball are some of the sports spectators enjoy. Golf and tennis buffs will find that in numerous areas of Washington these games are played year round.

Washington cities provide an abundance of cultural activities, from symphonies to folk dances. Some of the nation's best theatres and world class zoos can be found in the state.

Tourists are welcomed warmly to the folk festivals, salmon derbies, and county fairs that abound. It's a land for fun: one might attend the Bumbershoot, the Blazing Boots Fun Run, or Kn-Kanna-Xwa Day (Or get in to see a major league Seahawks football game or watch Mariners baseball!). Washington's bounty is truly a unique combination of metropolitan and natural delights.

You are the man or woman on the beach and Washington is about to unfold its wonders. Follow me, quietly, as I take you through the panorama of beauty that in 1889 became the 42nd state in the United States: Washington.

Point of Arches/Craig Tuttle

Cape Disappointment Lightbouse/Craig Tuttle

The Coast

Washington's coastline is sprinkled with small towns, scenic diversity, and a rich history. The lower portion of the coast, from Fort Canby on up to Grays Harbor, is popularly called Washington's Sunset Coast. From Grays Harbor northward, the coast becomes the Olympic Peninsula coast or the Olympic seashore.

The southwest corner of the coast is caught between the Columbia River, the Willapa Hills, and the long embracing arm of Willapa Bay. This corner is a western version of Cape Cod, with Victorian subtleties and an abundance of fishing boats, shipwrecks, and clams. It is a region of historic beginnings and cultural attractions.

Chinook Indian villages lined both the Columbia River and Willapa Bay before the nineteenth century. Cape Disappointment, where Fort Canby was later built, was the Chinook's favorite viewpoint on the ocean. Scarborough Hill was where they held canoe burials. Today the hill is a popular location for picnics and tours. Early excavation around the Fort Canby-Scarborough Hill site unearthed the Chinook burial hordes of glass, stoneware bowls, beads, cooking utensils, silver jewelry, and various other treasured items they had accumulated in trade. English and Spanish coins dating back to 1773 were found, as were eight-sided fifty-dollar slugs.

Long Beach Peninsula is recognized as the longest beach on earth. Perhaps its most unique feature is that its long stretch of ocean beach can be safely driven upon year round. The driveable portions are designated Washington highways. Although the ocean waters beckon invitingly, the ocean here is actually quite treacherous because of undertows and cross currents. The only close spot safe for swimmers can be found at Waikiki Beach in Fort Canby State Park. Long Beach, like many other areas of the Pacific Coast, offers the simple joys of exploring, hiking, or beachcombing for driftwood and glass floats. The sandy soils offer another advantage: they support the number one agricultural crop, cranberries.

Long Beach Peninsula is known for having some of the best oysters in the world. The harvesting of oysters is the major industry in communities such as Nahcotta and Oysterville. Although it is illegal for the public to harvest oysters in these areas, both crabbing and clamming are permitted without licensing. Good freshwater fishing on the peninsula can be found at Loomis Lake, the site of a state park, Island Lake on Cranberry Road, or O'Neil Lake at Fort Canby State Park. For salmon fishing and bottom fishing, boat moorages and charters are available at Nahcotta, Chinook, and Ilwaco.

When you're not out fishing, you'll want to visit the two historic state parks on the peninsula. Fort Columbia State Park is located between Chinook and the Astoria bridge and houses a collection of early marine displays and historical artifacts along with an art museum. The Lewis and Clark Interpretive Center is located on Cape Disappointment at Fort Canby State Park. Artifacts and exhibits describe the explorers' travels.

Out in the fresh air, gulls, cranes, herons, egrets, bitterns, and sandpipers draw birdwatchers while jasper, agates, basalt, and other rocks give the Pacific Coast notable appeal to rock hounds. Whatever your fancy, you'll find the exploring is made easy since beach trails and camping spots are plentiful on Long Beach Peninsula.

The Grays Harbor area, farther north, offers renowned deep sea fishing with salmon capping the list of several sports fish. Local canneries pack salmon, tuna, and oysters. Because Grays Harbor can accommodate ocean-going vessels, Hoquiam and Aberdeen have become important lumber and food product shipping centers. Willapa Harbor, close by, also serves ocean-bound ships.

South of Hoquiam and Aberdeen, there is a swampy area that abounded in native cranberries during the pioneer period. The berries are now produced commercially. Where cranberry bogs are missing, the grass is sufficiently abundant for local farmers to graze herds of dairy cattle.

Hugging the coastline north of Grays Harbor is Copalis Beach, "home of the razor clam." It is probably the greatest razor clam beach in the world. Ocean City, Ocean Shores, Moclips and Pacific Beach have other attractions. The main rivers feeding into this area, the Humptulips, Copalis, and the Quinault, provide steelhead and salmon fishing in season. You can also visit cranberry farms, salmon hatcheries, and tree farms.

Past these small beach towns lies the Quinault Indian Reservation. The Quinault region is best for seeing the rain forest by car, because US 101 travels through it. Queets, at the tip of the reservation, is an Indian village you will travel through if you stay on US 101. Access to other areas of the reservation are regulated by the Indians.

From Queets, the highway parallels the coast, hugging it or eleven miles. This strip is best explored by hiking from the highway. Despite the road, there are few signs of civilization and scenery remains much as it was when Washington was first discovered.

Stretching through the Olympic strip of the coast are the Hoh River and the Hoh Indian Reservation. The Hoh River valley shelters a rare and magnificent rain forest.

A wilderness site popular with hikers is Toleak Point, which lies six miles south of La Push. It is easily reached by hikers though they must be wary of headlands. Two of the headlands can be skirted at low tide, but at high tide, hikers must be prepared for a climb. Hiking efforts are worthwhile not only for the beautiful scenery, but for the chance to view bald eagles, as Toleak Point is one of the few remaining sanctuaries for the eagles.

Nahcotta, Washington/Steve Terrill

Quillayute Indian Reservation is home to the small fishing village of La Push. The natives cater to tourists, offering Indian articles for sale and renting charter boats for the fine salmon fishing off the coast. Cape Alava, like La Push, is located within the coastal strip of the Olympic National Park. Unlike La Push, it is not accessible by road. The experienced hiker can reach it from the four miles of trails that extend from the end of the road at Ozette. Cape Alava is the westernmost point in the three Pacific Coast states. Though Cape Flattery is commonly acknowledged as holding that distinction, Cape Alava actually holds the honor by a few hundred feet of clinging rock. At low tide, a small island is linked to Cape Alava by a sandspit. Spherical rocks, called "cannonball" rocks, are the unexplainable inhabitants of this small island called Indian, or Cannonball, Island.

One of the most beautiful views off the coast is Point of Arches. Rocks and rock islets scattered offshore have been sculpted into magnificent forms by the ever-present pounding waves. Tidepools and arches are explorable at low tide.

Cape Flattery provides breathtaking views of Tatoosh Island, Hole-In-The-Wall, Vancouver Island, and the Pacific Coastline. It is accessible by a thirty minute hike down a wooded trail.

Scenery is as varied as activities along Washington's Pacific Coast as the gallery of Washington scenes depicted in this book attests.

San Juan Island Sunset/Craig Tuttle

Olympic Peninsula

Washington's Olympic Peninsula contains some of the finest attractions to be found in the state.

If you begin at the southwestern tip of the Peninsula, you will start your travels near Grays Harbor. This harbor offers some of the best deep sea fishing in the world. Westport, which dots the map on the harbor's southern tip, is one of the largest sport fishing marinas on the West Coast.

The main highway, US 101, travels inland from Grays Harbor, gliding past small towns until it enters the Olympic National Forest. From there, US 101 begins its detour around the uppermost portion of the Quinault Indian Reservation. Before you take that inland jaunt though, don't forget the little towns and cities hugging the coastline. They are worth an excursion off the main highway.

Once back on US 101, you'll be skirting close to Lake Quinault. Lake Quinault Lodge is located on the south shore road. It is a rustic yet modern lodge tucked into the deep woods near this isolated, beautiful lake.

From the northwestern tip of the Quinault Reservation to Cape Alava, you'll be in the Pacific Coast area of Olympic National Park. Highway 101 will take you through the park as far as the Hoh River, which runs through the only coniferous rain forest in the world. If you enjoy hiking, the Hoh River Valley Trail follows the river and allows a walk through the most awesome remainder of beautiful virgin forest in the United States. The lush forests are dominated by Douglas fir, Sitka spruce, western red cedar, and hemlock. Gigantic spruce trees grow 300 feet tall and mosses drape the trees.

Further north is the city of Forks, originally called Indian Prairie. According to legend, the Indians living in the area burned the prairie every fall to provide better grazing for deer and elk. In 1878, Indian Prairie was purchased from the Indians by settlers. The price: one cow and one bowl of flour. The town's later name came from the settlers' familiar expression "meet me at the forks," since the town was situated at the meeting point of the Calawah and Bogachiel Rivers. The city of Forks also lies within fifteen miles of six world famous rivers for steelhead fishing. Headquarters for the Olympic National Forest and Olympic National Park is located just five miles north of Forks.

Five unique resorts are located within Olympic National Park. Sol Duc Hot Springs was once a famous spa for the wealthy until it burned in 1916. Today it boasts a new lodge and cabins plus three hot sulphur pools and a large fresh water swimming pool. It is a relaxing retreat. Lake Crescent Lodge is on the southern shore of beautiful Lake Crescent, where fishing, boating, swimming, and water-skiing are favored pastimes. Photographers find it to be an especially lovely haven. Thirty-five miles south of Forks is the Kalaloch Lodge. With its picturesque setting on the Pacific Ocean, it is perfect for watching an ocean sunset, for beachcombing, or clamming. Already mentioned is the magnificent Lake Quinault, and certainly not to be forgotten is the Quillayute Indian Reservation. Its beaches are strewn with driftwood of fascinating textures and designs. While on the reservation, you might charter a boat for a fishing trip, or, in early spring, whale watching provides an unusual form of entertainment. Quillayute Days, held each August, offer the rare opportunity to watch exciting Indian canoe races on the Quillayute River. While watching the races, have a meal featuring salmon that Indians have cooked their traditional way.

Cape Flattery is the northwestern-most point of the continental United States. It provides views of Tatoosh Island, Hole-In-The-Wall, Vancouver Island, and the Pacific Coastline. A thirty-minute hike gets you there.

Located in the northwestern corner of the Olympic Peninsula are the towns of Clallam Bay, Neah Bay, and Sekiu, the charter fishing headquarters for the

Strait of Juan de Fuca. Visitors from all over the country depart from Sekiu's docks to fish for King and Silver salmon and other species of fish. The Makah Museum and Cultural Center at nearby Neah Bay is home to several thousand cultural artifacts from the Cape Alava archaeological digs at Lake Ozette. This collection represents the largest collection of pre-contact American Indian artifacts in the world. A National Park campground is maintained at Lake Ozette, which is the third largest lake in the state. This is the trailhead to the archeological digs at Cape Alava.

On the north end of Clallam Bay lies The Sisters, a large cluster of rocks famous for its understated elegance. Just beyond The Sisters stretches a beach that is often strewn with Indian artifacts and fossils.

Ahh . . . and then we have Port Angeles. It is a paradise of majestic beauty. The Olympic Mountains, the Olympic National Park, the Strait of Juan de Fuca, and the expanses of the Pacific Ocean that surround it created its fame for being one of the most scenic areas in the Pacific Northwest. Port Angeles provides many family activities including ''touching tanks'' in the undersea exhibits at the Marine Lab. Port Angeles is the access point to one of the most scenic areas of the Olympic National Park, Hurricane Ridge, 5200 feet above sea level. Hurricane Ridge offers wildlife sightings, naturalist walks, park orientation talks, recreational activities, and a year-round lodge. Downhill and cross-country skiing and guided snowshoe walks are offered at the park on winter weekends.

Port Townsend, centrally located on Puget Sound, has been designated a National Historic District and is considered the finest example of a Victorian seacoast town north of San Francisco. Seventy Victorian residences and buildings are located there along with old forts, museums, and parks of historical note. Port Townsend, in early September, hosts the Wooden Boat Festival which seafarers, chantey singers, marine craftspeople, tourists, and locals attend.

Bremerton, further in on Puget Sound, is the site of the Puget Sound Naval Shipyard, the largest naval installation in the Pacific Northwest. Numerous state parks are within short driving distance of Bremerton. Poulsbo, nearby, preserves its Scandinavian heritage with the annual celebration of Norwegian Independence Day.

Rounding out our circular route of the Olympic Peninsula, we come to Shelton, Washington. Because of the many evergreens raised here, it is known as the Christmas Tree Capital Of The World. Shelton is located on the Hood Canal, a spectacular waterway whose marine waters produce stable annual returns of King, Chum, and Silver salmon as well as clams, oysters, crab, and the famous, huge, Hood Canal shrimp. Its temperate waters provide pleasurable hours of skin-diving and snorkeling. The marine life is abundant.

Untouched upon in our travels around the Olympic Peninsula are the listings of many small historical sites, roadside parks, and countless activities the countryside provides. The area is too profuse in delightful visiting spots to begin to list them all. You, my friend, have much to explore.

Puget Sound

Puget Sound, the deep inlet of the eastern North Pacific, indents Northwest Washington State and stretches south for 100 miles. Hood Canal is a large western extension of the Sound and Skagit, Snohomish, and Duwamish Waterways enter the Sound from the east. Each of these waterways are navigable for a portion of their lengths. Excellent deepwater harbors abound, too, including those of Seattle, Tacoma, Everett, and Port Townsend. These harbors serve as outports for the wealth of products that are exported. The mild climate and relatively flat farming terrain have drawn the bulk of the state's population to the Puget Sound area along with the lion's share of the state's manufacturing.

Not in this telling is the hint of the sheer magical beauty of Puget Sound, for the Sound supports everything from large cities to quaint villages to secluded private inlets amongst the San Juan Islands. It is on one hand a sheltered playground, on the other an old-hand at big business.

The San Juan Islands, if you really want to be a stickler about it, aren't officially part of the Sound, but to us unofficial exlorers they fit right in. While location-wise they're only a few miles from the main centers of population for the state, they are in many ways as far removed as the Carribean. They lie, as the travel brochures are wont to say, "like rough-cut emeralds scattered on an inland sea." Indeed, they are a beautiful sight, full of little nooks and coves awaiting exploration. By sailboat or ferry you can reach a variety of resorts on the islands. Some are small and rustic and others more elegant, but all offer a peaceful departure that is only found in a few other places.

In the islands' largest town, Friday Harbor on San Juan, there are an assortment of quaint little shops. On Orcas, don't miss the view from Mt. Constitution.

Alki Point Lighthouse/Craig Tuttle

24

It offers a dazzling panoramic view of Washington, British Columbia, and the other islands of the San Juans.

On the Washington mainland east of the San Juan Islands is the city of Bellingham. Situated between Mt. Baker to the east, and the San Juans and Pacific Ocean to the west, the scenic beauty of the area is world renowned. Recreation in the Bellingham area includes the same seaside activities many of the Washington coastal areas are famous for including scuba diving, clamming, oyster hunting, and inner tidal exploration. Inland, county parks and city parks offer tennis, swimming, golfing, picnicking, playgrounds, baseball, indoor and outdoor rifle ranges, and a broad range of other activities. The beautiful waters of Bellingham Bay and the inland waterways of the Sound and the numerous San Juan islands are an entrancing paradise for sailors and boaters. The city is popular with outdoorsmen because of the unlimited camping and hiking that abounds in the immense reaches of the National Forests, National Parks, and public and county parks. The Nooksack River along with other area streams and lakes, offers fishermen superb catches of salmon, steelhead, and cutthroat trout. For skiing enthusiasts, there's Mt. Baker, a splendid ski area that has a good snow base nine months of the year.

Anacortes is known as the gateway to the San Juan Islands and is a departure point for a ferry to Victoria, B.C. Its port encompasses sixty square miles, including the city of Anacortes itself, and several of the outlying San Juan Islands. A bit of Indian history is represented in the city's Washington Park where the featured attraction is a thirty-foot-tall totem pole carved into various animals representative of the major Indian tribes in the Northwest. Another little piece of history, the W.J. Preston, a stern-wheeler work boat, is owned by the city of Anacortes and is open for tours.

One of the most beautiful and spectacular areas in the U.S. is Deception Pass State Park on Whidbey Island. The park has four miles of sandy beaches and over

1700 acres of virgin forests for hiking. The Deception Pass bridge offers a bird's-eye view of the boiling rapids that surge through the narrow channel. Picnicking and camping facilities are available at the park and a multitude of activities can be enjoyed. Further south on Whidbey Island is Oak Harbor, the site of the U.S. Naval Air Station, Ault Field. Floral gardens and a historical museum are just a couple of the pleasures tourists enjoy at Oak Harbor.

Coupeville, south of Oak Harbor, is the showcase for 48 authentic falsefront buildings and pioneer homes dating back to 1890.

In the section on the Olympic Peninsula, Port Townsend and Bremerton have already been discussed, so let's move on towards the city of Everett. Everett is home to the largest marina north of Marina Del Ray. Ships traveling from there depart to such exotic ports as Singapore and Hong Kong and their cargoes may be made up of apples, logs, or aluminum ore.

And then we have Seattle, a city stirring with excitement. The waterfront along Elliott Bay shelters more than 2,000 commercial deep sea vessels. Pier 59 on Waterfront Park is home to the world class Seattle Aquarium. A short walk from the aquarium is Pike Place Market, the only continuously operating farmer's market in America. With over 250 shops and restaurants and the artwork of more than 200 artisans, the market deserves at least a day of your time. For theatre buffs, some of the best theatre in the West, along with fantastic sports action, is available in Seattle's Kingdome. There's even an international district that highlights the diverse cultures of Korea, China, and Japan. And one must not forget the Space Needle, constructed for 1962s World Fair and now utilized as a regional cultural center.

Tacoma shares fame with Seattle in that it is one of the ten largest natural deep-water ports in the world. Tacoma's Point Defiance Park offers a look at the Pacific Rim animal species, or visit the old British Fort Nisqually for its reconstruction of the old "54-40 or fight" days when both Great Britain and the United States claimed the territory.

Our last stop on the Puget Sound tour is Olympia, the capital of Washington. Olympia is, as are all the Puget Sound cities, a beautifully laid-out and well-preserved piece of history combined with bustling commerce and signs of an even more energetic future. Known as the "Pearl of Puget Sound," Olympia is a deep-sea port. It is also the starting point of the Olympic Highway, which circles the Olympic National Park and the Olympic National Forest. As the state capital, it features the State Capitol Museum, which was the 1920s mansion of the Lord Family. The museum preserves the native American, pioneer, territorial, and state government history of Washington.

There, though briefly, we have toured 'round the Puget Sound area of Washington. While words alone are insufficient, perhaps coupled with the beautiful photographs of this most photogenic location, you will get a taste of the magnificent splendor of the Puget Sound.

Gig Harbor/Gary Greene

(Opposite) Deception Pass/Steve Terrill

The Mountains

Geographically, Washington is a state of diversity. This springs from the seven distinct regions its mountains create.

The most dominant of the mountain ranges are the rugged and snow-capped Cascade Mountains, lying east of the Puget Sound region. Towering above the range are Mount Rainier, Mount Adams, Mount Baker, and Glacier Peak, all of volcanic origin. Mount St. Helens, which once shared their lofty companionship, erupted in 1980, changing her stature.

The Cascades were named by U.S. explorers Meriwether Lewis and William Clark in 1806. They sighted the range from the Columbia River Gorge and named it after the great cascades they found near the gorge. The forests of the Cascades remain much the same as they did then, for with the exception of the peaks above the timberline, the entire Cascade Range is heavily wooded. Its reaches lie under the auspices of state and national forest protection acts.

Mt. Rainier is the highest peak in the Cascade chain. Two thousand years ago, Mt. Rainier was an active volcano; today the mountain is surrounded by the largest single-peak glacier system in the United States. Twenty-six glaciers radiate outward from the summit. The 100 square miles of the mountain's body are wrapped in a protective cloak of conservation known as Mt. Rainier National Park, and a beautiful park it is. There are thick forests of coniferous trees, picturesque, crystal clear lakes, rolling meadows, and a profusion of flowers and wildlife. The mountain received its title when George Vancouver, the English explorer, sighted it in 1792 and named it after Peter Rainier, a fellow navigator.

Climbing Rainier's summit is a challenge that attracts climbers from afar. Top-notch guide services are available. The lower reaches of the mountain are packed with hiking trails and camping spots so those who are less interested in reaching the summit can enjoy the marvelous scenery further down. The best time for camping and hiking is during the summer months, for by mid-July most of the snow has abandoned the trails.

Winter in the Cascades can be formidable with snow-falls of twenty feet in the higher elevations, but these same snows warm the hearts of skiing enthusiasts. The Cascades shelter a number of extremely fine ski areas, among them Mt. Baker, just 56 miles from Bellingham, in the northern part of the state. In the central Cascades, skiers enjoy Alpental, Stevens Pass, Snoqualmie, Ski Acres, Pacific West, and Mission Ridge. Crystal Mountain and White Pass ski areas are two other superb spots and are located not far from Mt. Rainier's shadow.

Mount St. Helens is the most active volcano in the Cascade Range. St. Helen's most recent major eruption began on March 20, 1980, and measured 4.1 on the Richter Scale. For two months small steam and ice eruptions occurred, then on May 18th a 5.0 earthquake caused the entire north side of the mountain to give way in a rolling torrent of rock, mud, and ice which traveled for fifteen miles. Following the avalanche were explosions that blew millions of tons of ash, ice, and rock into the air, killing everything in their path. Since that time smaller eruptions have occurred, building miniature lava domes on the crater's floor. Periodically, the mountain gasps and steam can be seen, but she is calmer, allowing close-up inspection. Access by car, tour bus, or private flights is possible.

An eruption 1,900 years ago was less explosive in nature than recent activity, but it formed another area worthy of exploration—Ape Cave. With a length of 12,810 feet, it is the longest intact lava tube in the continental United States. The cave was named for the St. Helens Apes, a speleological organization that first explored it.

St. Helens, Ape Cave, and the surrounding area are part of the Gifford Pinchot National Forest. Like all of the Washington forests, Gifford Pinchot

offers enthusiasts a wealth of hiking, fishing, camping, mountain climbing, swimming, boating, river rafting, berry picking, and picture taking opportunities. Snowmobilers and skiers are drawn to the area in winter.

In the southern part of the state, the Willapa Hills run along the coast from Grays Harbor to the Columbia River. This land is much gentler than the Cascades, and its open, rolling hills are less wooded.

The protection of the Willapa Hills and the Olympics on the west and the Cascades on the east forms the third geographical area, Puget Sound. This lowland region owes its mild climate to the shelter these giant protectors have provided. That climate has assisted in gaining this area its wealth of population.

The Columbia Basin region covers the Central Washington area outlined by the Cascade Mountains on the west, the Okanogan Mountains to the north, and the Blue Mountains to the south. The Okanogan Mountains alone compose yet another region. The Okanogans are an extension of the Rocky Mountains. Though less rugged than the Cascade and Olympic mountains, peaks do range from 4,000 to 8,000 feet. Most of the minerals and metals mined in Washington come from this region.

In the southeast, the Blue Mountain region is lightly settled. The mountains offer visitors striking contrasts in scenery as the Blues have been molded by wind and water to become a geologically diverse area. There are Alpine hills and deserts, sculpted hills, and deep canyons.

Clear across the state in the northwest corner, reside the Olympic Mountains. These mountains, combined with the Pacific as a border on the west, form the boundaries of the seventh and final region, the Olympic Peninsula. The Spanish navigator, Juan Perez, sighted the mountains in 1774. In 1788, John Mears, an English voyager, named the highest peak Mt. Olympus because it appeared, like the Greek Mt. Olympus, to be a home fit for the gods.

At 7,965 feet, Olympus is the highest mountain, but Mts. Anderson and Deception also top 7,000 feet. The range holds about 60 glaciers. On the

Paradise Inn/Mark Windom

(Opposite) *Mt. Shuksan/Mark Windom*

Olympics' western slopes, where annual precipitation can reach up to 140 inches in places, lies a lush rain forest in which conifers can reach heights of nearly 300 feet with diameters of eight feet. These forests are made up predominantly of Douglas fir, Sitka spruce, western red cedar, and hemlock. The forest floor is thick with mosses and huge fungi. The eastern slopes are less thickly forested and many pretty lakes and meadows can be found.

The Olympic National Park was established in 1938 to preserve these mountains and their breathtaking scenery. They, like the other mountains of Washington, provide a wealth of beauty and resources for the state that can be appreciated not only by its residents, but by any who travel the state, whether in person or through pictures of its captivating scenery.

(Opposite) Tatoosh Range/Craig Tuttle

Central Washington

Central Washington State, if a rough map were drawn, could best be defined as the area that falls between the east slope of the Cascade Range and west of that portion of the Columbia River which runs north to south. Central Washington's northern and southern borders are fringed by Canada and Oregon. The cities that fall within this strip are surrounded by independent farmlands and orchards. Wenatchee, Yakima, Ellensburg, Chelan, and Okanogan orchards and farms supply enough fruit for both state use and for shipping to other areas all over the United States. What has given these cities independence and prosperity are the dams on the Columbia and Yakima Rivers. They provide the water necessary for growing the famous Washington apples and enable Central Washington to produce a supply of fruits and vegetables ample enough for much of America, even the world. In addition, the Columbia dams have made ports of many of the inland cities and the power supply created by the dams has increased the industrial potential for the area.

The Okanogan Highlands, considered part of Central Washington, are an extension of the Rockies and contain most of the minerals and metals mined in the state. The city, sharing the same name as the Highlands, sits on sage-covered foothills with pine forests as a backdrop. Okanogan's front porch is the Okanogan River which forms the western boundary of the Colville Indian Reservation. The area around the city provides fishing, camping, hiking, backpacking, snowmobiling, and skiing.

Naturally, nearby Omak, known for its apple harvests, offers many of the same outdoor activities. The city's name is derived from an Indian word meaning "good medicine" and the town's healthful, dry climate, with more than 300 days of sunshine in an average year, supports that legacy.

For a change of pace, visit Chelan. It's nestled in the Cascade Mountains on the banks of Lake Chelan, which glistens like a Norwegian fjord. The sixty-mile-long lake lies in a glacial trough that was dammed up long ago by a huge terminal moraine. The Indian name for Chelan is "deep water" and the lake's depth of 1,600 feet lends credence to its ancient name. The "Lady of the Lake" launch makes a daily trip from Chelan at the lower end of the lake to Stehekin at the head of the lake. The launch makes many stops, as it is a mail carrier as well as a tourist boat, and one may depart for explorations along the way or travel the full fifty-five miles to Stehekin. Stehekin is approachable only by boat, seaplane, or by traveling the trails over the Cascades. Amid a gorgeous landscape with peaks of 8,500 to 9,500 feet, it is a secluded natural area protected from the outside world because of the specific prohibition against road construction by Congress when it created the Lake Chelan National Recreation Area. In addition to the attractions the lake offers, winter brings downhill skiing at nearby Echo Valley and Mission Ridge. Nordic skiing, snowshoeing, and snowmobiling are enticements of these areas.

East of the Lake Chelan National Recreation Area and north of the city of Chelan is the little community of Twisp. Twisp, which is the Indian word for yellowjacket, is situated in the charming Methow Valley. Rafters shoot the Methow River, and the high country with its tranquil meadows carpeted with wild-flowers offers trails for hikers and horseback riders.

Leavenworth, northwest of Wenatchee, billed as the Apple Capital of the World, is the mirror of a Bavarian village. Interesting shops, many offering remarkable arts and crafts, line the streets.

Yakima is the largest and most prosperous of the east-slope cities. It is the hub of the Yakima Valley and is a fertile farming area with lush fruit orchards, hop fields, and vineyards. The area ranks first in the United States for production of hops, apples, and mint. Tourism is Yakima's second largest industry. The area is

Balsamroot and lupine in the Klickitat Valley/Craig Tuttle

Wenatchee National Forest/Gary Greene

Wenatchee River/Rollin Geppert

also the second largest for wine production in the United States. Small produce stands, just off the highways, offer fresh fruits and vegetables for the traveler.

The Yakima Indian Reservation stretches east and south of Yakima. In Toppenish, the Yakima Nation Cultural Center offers a wide array of Indian artifacts for viewing.

Ellensburg puts its name on the map with rock collectors because of a highly valued agate, the Ellensburg Blue, found only in this area. East of Ellensburg is the Ginkgo Petrified Forest on the great Columbia's bank. Also near Ellensburg is Olmstead Park, listed on the National Register of Historic Sites and maintained much as it was when founded in the 1870s.

Stretching west from the Columbia through the Yakima Indian Reservation toward the Cascades, are the gradually rising slopes of Horse Heaven Hills. It's a rather remote area that is gradually becoming more prosperous because of increased rainfall. The name Horse Heaven Hills was acquired because of the herds of wild horses that roamed there, and it is said that remnants of those great herds still graze upon its grasses.

There are many of the lovely lakes, recreational areas, and small towns left unexplored in this rendition of Central Washington. Because this portion of the state has a great number of sunny days, an abundance of water, and hundreds of activities and excursions for the taking, it is often the tourist's first choice of locations when visiting Washington.

This is one of my favorite photos here. Though our area is flatter, it has this feel.

Winter on the Palouse/Charley Gurche

Mt. Rainier/Rollin Geppert

Molbak's Poinsettias, Woodinville/Gary Greene

(Opposite) Tulip Fields, Mt. Vernon/Gary Greene

Liberty Bell Mountain, North Cascade National Park/Dave Logan

(Opposite) Mt. Baker/Steve Terrill

Pike Place Market, Seattle/Mark Windom

(Opposite) Hot Air Balloon Festival at night; Wenatchee/Craig Tuttl

Olympic Peninsula/Rollin Geppert

Mountain Goat, Hurricane Ridge/Steve Terrill

Cherry Blossoms, U of W/Gary Greene

Fall Cottonwood/Craig Tuttle

(Opposite) Mt. Adams, Glenwood Valley/Larry Geddis

Our southern border, the Columbia River at sunrise/Craig Tuttle

Southern Washington

To tour Southern Washington in this account is to travel that part of the state that edges the Columbia River. It makes matters easier to designate this general region as "south" because to draw away from the river is to fall into a different geographical area. The banks of the Columbia offer breathtaking scenic views and communities lining the river are naturally enhanced by its presence. Commercial vessels and brilliantly colored sailing boats are as much a part of it as the fish that swim its waters. In the Columbia Gorge, windsurfing conditions are the very finest in the world. While novices can find a sheltered site to learn the tecniques of windsurfing, experts will find that the opposing currents provide challenges second to none, because of this, the area draws expert windsurfers from all over the world.

At the rugged and forested mouth of the great river is the town of Ilwaco, with moorage for over 1,000 boats. When you bring in your catch of salmon or other fish, canneries in the area will can, freeze, or pack the fish for transportation home.

Upriver from Ilwaco is Megler. The next 50 miles or so, the river winds through rural countryside. Where the river turns south towards Portland, Oregon, lie the cities of Longview and Kelso, known for their wood processing. The Weyerhaeuser company headquarters are located nearby.

Vancouver is the first city of size among the Columbia River towns. While it is a progressive, rapidly growing city, visiting its Fort Vancouver is like taking a step back in time. The fort has been re-created on the site where Hudson's Bay Company established its trading fort in 1825. The buildings were originally constructed as part of the Pacific Northwest's first military post. Fort Vancouver is open seven days a week, year round. National Park Service Rangers provide guided tours.

If you enjoy fishing, wet your line at the city boat launch in Vancouver to hook salmon, sturgeon, trout, steelhead, and shad. If watching these efforts is more your cup of tea, the city's waterfront restauraunts offer superb dining and you can watch as sailing boats, commercial vessels, and the Columbia River Stern-wheeler glide by.

Close to the city is Vancouver Lake, which is gaining in popularity with windsurfers and is considered a top fishing spot. A short drive from Vancouver is the 800 foot sheer-walled monolith known as Beacon Rock. It is the largest such formation in the United States, yet it is easily climbed for a magnificent view of the Columbia Gorge. Adjacent to the monolith are a State Park and the lovely Hamilton Mountain Trail, enjoyable stopping places for families.

Of prime importance to the communites of Washington and Oregon is the Bonneville Dam, further upriver. It was the first of the dams built on the Columbia. Walkways and escalators allow visitors to see working parts of the dam. Also popular are the fish-viewing facility and the historical displays.

Stevenson is the next stop on the river and its Rock Creek Park is a pleasant retreat that houses a new outdoor museum. The Skamania County Historical Museum nearby houses the largest collection of rosaries in the world.

You can luxuriate in hot mineral baths from natural springs when you reach the Carson Hotel. North of the Carson area, splendid rafting and fishing possibili-ties abound on the Wind River, home of the largest tree nursery in the world. A trip up Wind River Canyon affords a magnificent view and for high suspense, pardon the pun, cross Wind River on the suspension bridge 250 feet over its waters.

Soon, the scenery begins to change as the Columbia highway crosses the summit of the Cascades and the forests become more open on this, the east slope.

Maryhill Museum/Larry Geddis

Beacon Rock/Craig Tuttle

Highway 141 heads north at the Bingen/White Salmon area towards the recreation area around Mt. Adams. Ice caves in the area were formed by violent volcanic action. Near Trout Lake some of these caves are easily accessible, though exploration is unguided. Also near Trout Lake is Indian Sacred Viewpoint. From this peaceful vantage point, the view of Mt. Adams is spectacular. In the area surrounding Trout Lake, from mid-August to mid-September, you can pick wild huckleberries until your buckets and bellies are full.

The White Salmon River that runs through the countryside is greatly favored by fishermen and white water rafters. Glimpses of a rapidly disappearing era are seen at the mouth of the river where there's an Indian fishing camp and where logs still shoot down the Broughton Log Fume, the last of its kind still in use in the United States. Located in White Salmon is the Gorge Heritage Museum.

Moving on up the Columbia, you'll pass Horsethief Lake State Park, near The Dalles Lock and Dam. The Dalles area has much to offer history buffs.

The road takes you on to the Maryhill Museum of Art and Maryhill State Park. Built by an eccentric millionaire, the mansion sits isolated on a high bluff. The lavish "Castle on the Columbia" contains a large Rodin Collection, a wide range of European art, and Indian artifacts. Two miles to the east, there is even a replica of Stonehenge. The Maryhill Park is a well-kept sanctuary of green with a tiny, historic church, an old steam engine, and the availability of fresh fruit in season. You might also wish to take Highway 97 north to visit the Goldendale Observatory and some of the other historic sights surrounding it.

Wherever you travel along this southern boundary of the Columbia, you will find its unparalleled beauty as awe-inspiring today as it was when the first explorers disembarked upon its shores.

Eastern Washington

Washington's eastern side falls on the "dry" side of the Cascade Mountain Range. Of course this boundary is imaginary, but there is a remarkable difference in this area compared to the "wet" side west of the Cascades. For our purposes we will go even further and designate the eastern region to be that area which falls east of the portion of the Columbia that travels from north to south.

Eastern Washington used to be like the images painted of frontier days: endless stretches of dry, open land for cattle grazing and sparse farmlands, with a rush of mining activity in the mountains. The dams, the Grand Coulee being the largest, have changed that scenario. They have turned a previously dry, desolate area into one that is varied and rich in its combination of crop production and high technology. Thousands of previously arid acres now produce wheatfields, row crops, orchards, and vineyards.

Of course, much of the past remains. The town of Republic in the northeast section grew up around an 1896 gold discovery and retains much of the mining town ambiance. Several old gold mines and ghost towns are located around Republic. In this same corner of the state you'll find Metaline Falls and nearby Boundary Dam. The largest limestone cavern in Washington, Gardner Cave, is close by at Crawford State Park. A host of small rivers and lakes abound in this part of Washington, among them, the Kettle and San Poil rivers and Long Lake, Fish Lake, and Swan Lake.

Lake Roosevelt is one of the lakes formed by the Grand Coulee Dam. The formation of the Grand Coulee took place millions of years ago when molten rock poured over a volcanic landscape. When the glaciers came, their melting formed coulees, or canyons, in these volcanic layers. The largest of these was the Grand Coulee. When progress came to Washington, the Grand Coulee Dam was built. A

Mt. Adams Wilderness/Craig Tuttle

*(Opposite) Southern Pacific's historic locomotive 4449 steams
through the Wenatchee valley/Craig Tuttle*

Woody Guthrie song calls it the "mightiest thing ever built by man." It formed Lake Roosevelt, a giant of a lake with over 660 miles of shoreline. It's just one of hundreds of lakes in the region which offer virtually any kind of water sport and plenty of fresh water fishing.

Spokane is the largest city of Eastern Washington and has perhaps benefited more than any other area from the hydroelectric projects. Known as the "Lilac City," Spokane was the site of the 1974 World's Fair. It is a large regional trade center that provides services to a number of surrounding counties and states, which justifies its being called the Heart of the Inland Empire. This empire stretches over counties and cities in Washington, Idaho, Montana, parts of western Canada and part of eastern Oregon.

Spokane is also a hub of activity. There are many wonderful places to visit and explore, among them, Spokane's renowned Manito Park. This lovely park features the Spokane-Nishinomiya Japanese Garden, with its atmosphere of quiet harmony. The rest of Manito Park is just as inviting. Eighteenth century-styled Duncan Gardens show an abundance of lilacs and roses, and a conservatory graces the lawns.

Finch Arboretum, a sixty-five acre botanical showcase, and the Corey Glen Rhododendron Gardens are other attractions.

History buffs will find Spokane packed with places to explore. There's the Museum of Native American Cultures, a five-level tower museum offering one of the most comprehensive collections of Indian art and artifacts ever gathered. The Cheney Cowles Museum is a noteworthy spot, too. It contains exhibits relating to the natural history, the geology, and the historical development of the Spokane area.

Children love, (adults, too), the Walk in the Wild, a 240 acre park site exhibiting many species of North American wildlife. The park features nature trails, parrot shows, and a petting zoo. Photographers love 17,000-acre Turnbull

National Wildlife Refuge, south of Spokane. The park can be driven through or walked through on numerous trails, or the varied migratory waterfowl in the park can be viewed from behind blinds for an even closer look.

A geological delight is Riverside State Park, near Spokane's city center. The Bowl and Pitcher lava rock formation and other volcanic outcroppings are landmarks of the park. Hiking trails and an equestrian area are other pluses and there's RV and camping facilities as well.

While these are just a sprinkling of the outdoor sites, there's so much more to do and see in Spokane. There are art film houses and numerous movie complexes along with top-notch regional and jazz performances. Restaurants overlook the Spokane River, and boutiques, designer shops, and galleries abound in the area.

Spokane makes it easy to view its attractions, for there are the Spokane Tour Train, gondola rides, or for something different, a "heli-jet" boat trip up the Spokane River to Spokane Falls with the return helicopter trip touring the Spokane downtown area.

Spokane's richness extends from the recreational paradise that surrounds it to its abundance of other natural resources and man-made opportunities.

The Turnbull National Wildlife Refuge south of Spokane is a tribute to wildlife conservation efforts. Its importance to the nesting and migrating waterfowl in the Pacific Flyway cannot be understated. Restored as closely as possible to their original states, the lakes and marshes of the refuge also support hundreds of other types of birds and mammals.

Ritzville's terrain is typical of Eastern Washington. The rolling hills, stretching for miles and miles, were formed millions of years ago when a giant glacial lake in Montana burst. Its waters rushed across all of east Washington in a very short time. Ritzville's hills now ripple with waves of wheat as far as you can see, come harvest time. The town is headquarters for the Wheat Growers Association.

This isn't our area, but very like it — both of these pages.

Palouse River Canyon/Rollin Geppert

(Opposite) Palouse Grain Fields/Rollin Geppert

Richland, Pasco, and Kennewick make up the area known throughout Washington as the Tri-Cities. The cities are located at the confluence of the Snake, Yakima, and Columbia rivers. With all this wealth of water, water related activities are naturally a large part of those cities' recreational draw. Numerous vineyards in the area have made it one of the top wine centers in the United States. The Hanford Science Center has helped to develop the area into a major center of technological industries.

Walla Walla, called the Cradle of Northwest History, was one of the first regions between the Rocky Mountains and the Cascades to be settled. Its historic beginnings are well documented in the fascinating Fort Walla Walla Museum displays. The Whitman Mission National Historic Site, in the city, depicts missionary frontier life in the early 1800s. The Whitman Mission was an important stop on the Oregon Trail. A rough translation of Walla Walla's Indian name is "valley of many waters."

When the wheatfields of Eastern Washington explode in golden yellow, almost every town holds its own harvest festival. There are square dancing, livestock shows, tractor pulls, and pageants from Clarkston to Colville.

As winter creeps in, skiers and snowmobilers are drawn by the thousands to the Blue Mountains. Horse-drawn sleigh rides through the Palouse, or the lighted boat parades on the Columbia near the Tri-Cities, are just some of the ways people celebrate life, no matter what the season, in Eastern Washington.

It would make a splendid vacation to tour all the places mentioned in this book, to visit each section of the state and partake of the beautiful sights and bountiful opportunities. Fitting in the amount of time it would take to travel the entire state, however, is something most people cannot do. For many of us, reading about the area and looking at the magnificent scenery of the state not only whets our appetite for travel, but gives us an idea of specific areas we can visit in the time we have available.

Whether you can travel the state, exploring at your leisure, or use this book as your sole passport, I hope you find the state of Washington to be as delightful and as lovely as I found it to be.

View from Mt. Spokane/Steve Terrill

Rear Cover/Craig Tuttle